Things That Sparkle

ACTIVITY BOOK

this book belongs to

Name:

Date:

Can you find me?

Circle all the fairies you can find!

Name:

Date:

Tracing Lines

Trace the lines to get the fairies into their houses.

Name: ______________________ Date: ______________________

Tracing Lines

Trace the lines to get the butterflies to their flowers.

Name: ______________________ Date: ______________________

Trace and Write

Trace the lines to create the letter.

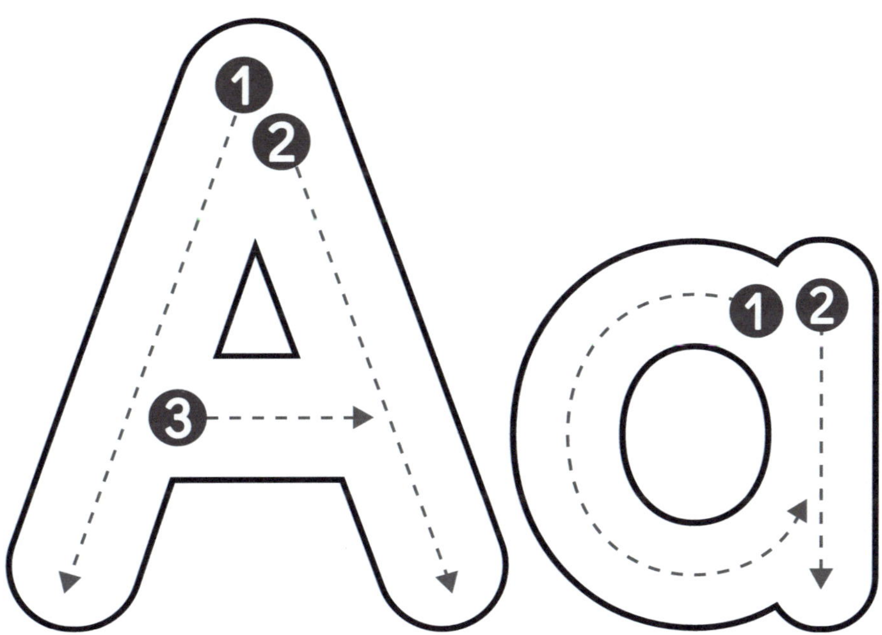

Circle each **A**.

W	A	N
A	X	V
A	A	N

Circle each **a**.

c	a	e
a	c	d
a	b	a

Name: ______________________ Date: ______________________

Tracing Circles

Trace the circles to draw the bubbles.

Bb

Bb

Name: ______________________ Date: ______________________

Color the Aa

Color the capital A's red and lower case a's blue.

A	a	A	A	a	A	a
A	A	a	A	A	a	A
a	A	a	A	A	a	A
A	a	A	a	A	A	a
A	a	A	a	A	a	A
a	A	a	a	a	A	A
A	A	A	a	A	a	a
a	A	a	A	a	a	A
A	a	A	a	A	a	A

Name: ______________________ Date: ______________________

Tracing Hearts

Trace the hearts to show how much the unicorn loves to prance.

Name: ______________________ Date: ______________________

Trace and Write

Trace the lines to create the letter.

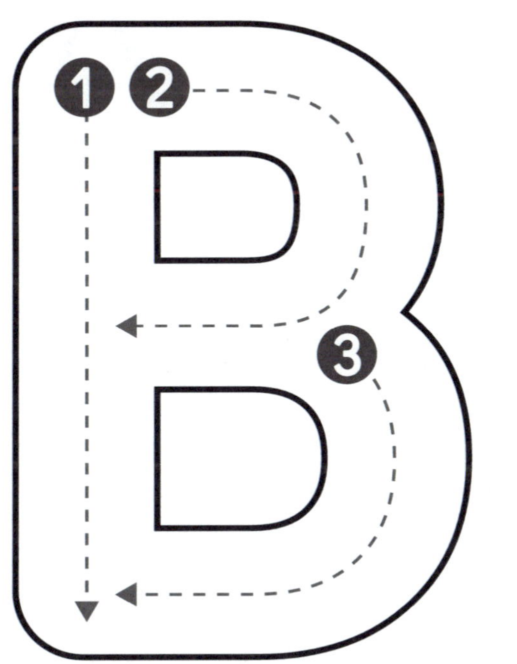

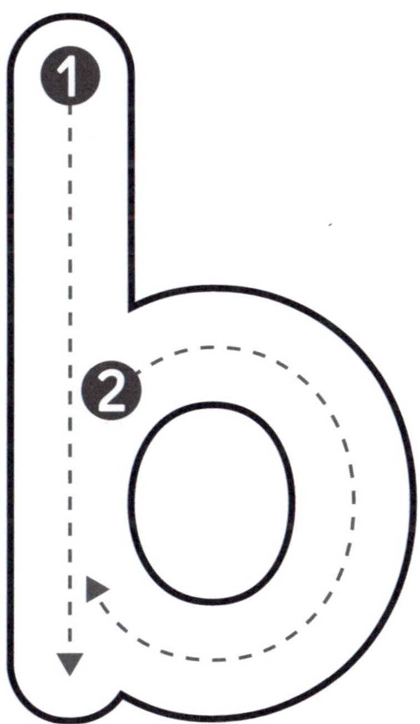

Circle each **B**.

A D B

P B G

B H B

Circle each **b**.

b e b

b n o

u y b

Name: ______________________ Date: ______________________

Star Numbers

Trace the numbers to count the stars.

Name: ______________________ Date: ______________________

Count and Circle

Circle the correct number of thing(s).

1	  

2	   
3	    
4	    
5	  
6	

Name: ______________________ Date: ______________________

Star ABC's

Trace the letters to complete the ABC's.

Name: ______________________ Date: ______________________

Color the Bb

Color the capital B's pink and lower case b's purple.

B b b B b B B

b b B B B b B

B b B b B b b

b b B b B b B

B B b b B B b

b B B B b b B

b b b b B B b

b B B B b B b

b b B b B B b

Name:

Date:

Trace and Write

Trace the lines to create the letter.

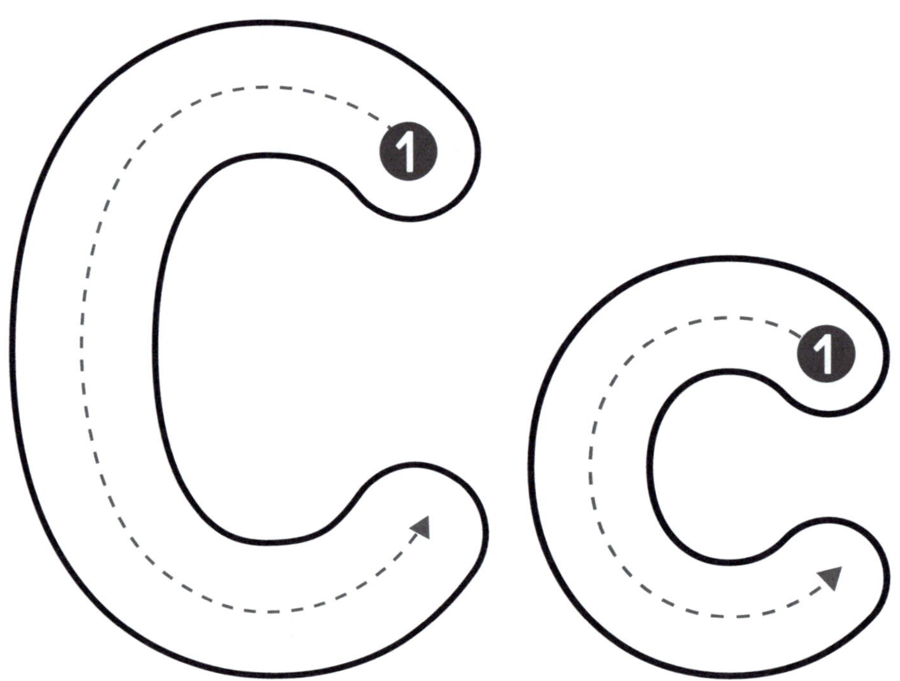

Circle each C.

E	D	C
A	C	B
C	F	C

Circle each c.

g	e	c
c	g	c
e	c	f

Name: ____________________ Date: ____________________

Tracing Lines

Trace the lines to help the mermaids get their treats.

Name: ______________________ Date: ______________________

Maze Fun!

Complete the maze to help the fairy get to her house.

Name: ______________________ Date: ______________________

Trace and Write

Trace the lines to create the letter.

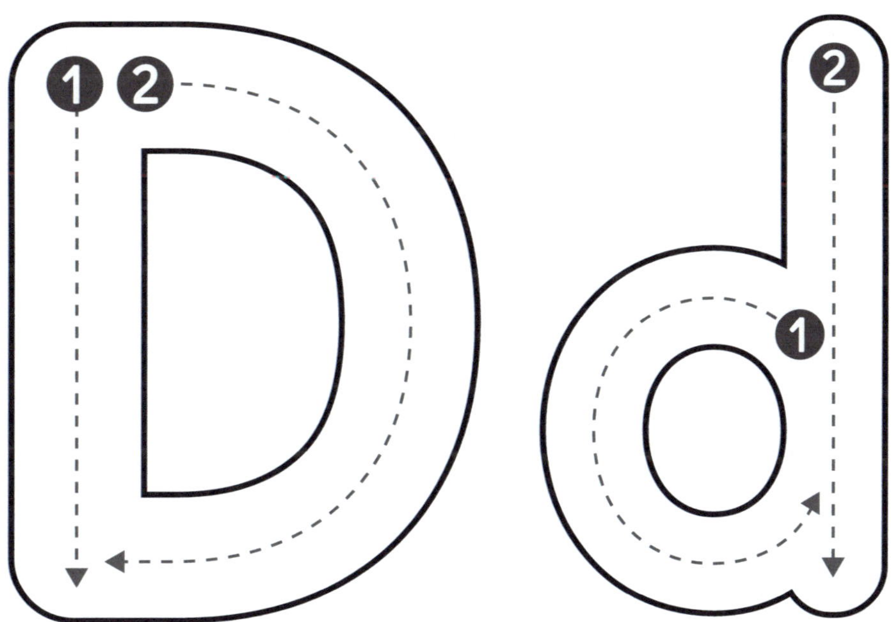

Circle each **D**.

D	G	G
C	D	D
F	D	C

Circle each **d**.

b	d	g
e	d	d
d	b	c

Name: ______________________ Date: ______________________

Color the Dd

Color the capital D's red and lower case d's blue.

D	d	d	d	D	d	D
d	D	d	D	D	D	d
d	d	d	d	d	D	D
D	D	D	D	d	d	D
d	D	D	d	D	D	d
D	d	d	D	D	d	D
D	d	D	d	d	D	d
d	d	D	D	d	d	d
D	D	D	d	D	D	D

Name:

Date:

Tracing Rectangles

Trace the rectangles.

Name: ____________________ Date: ____________________

Trace and Write

Trace the lines to create the letter.

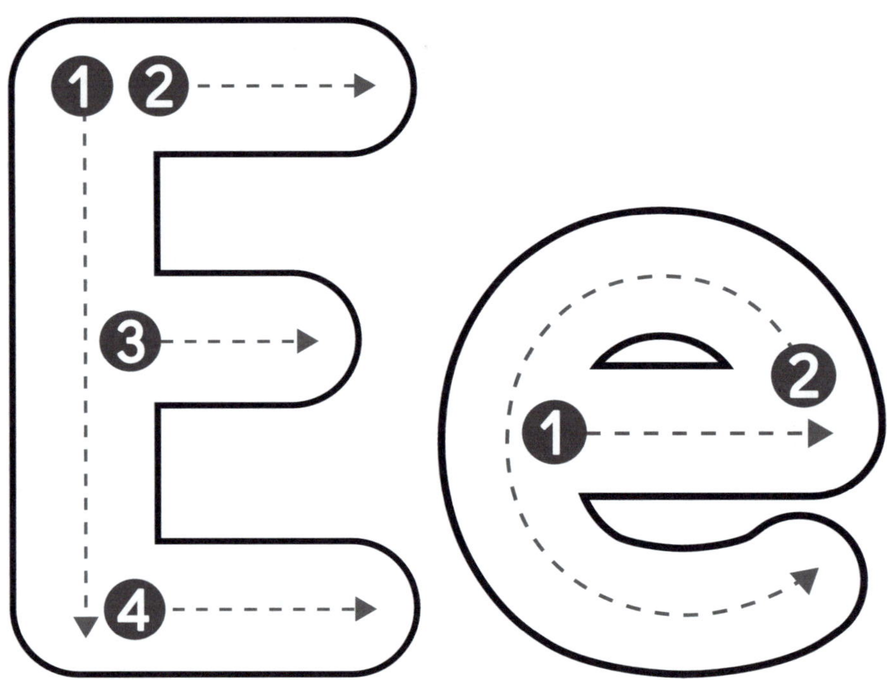

Circle each **E**.

D E E

D G P

G E D

Circle each **e**.

e p b

e b e

h e p

Name: ______________________ Date: ______________________

Tracing Letters

Name: ______________________ Date: ______________________

Shape Matching

These sneaky carriages are pretending to be grey!
Draw a line to match each hiding carriage.

Name: ______________________ Date: ______________________

Trace and Write

Trace the lines to create the letter.

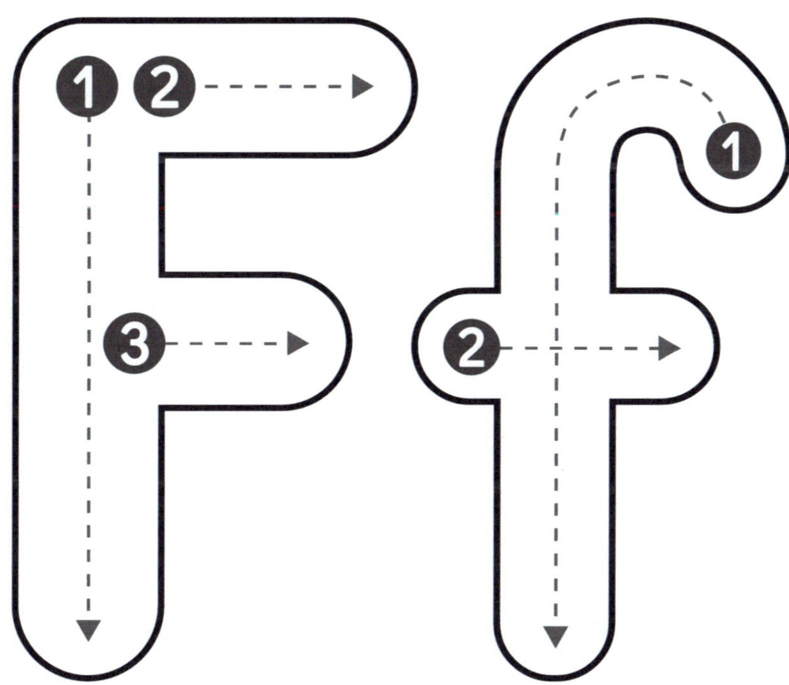

Circle each **F**.

F	C	I
D	H	F
F	A	F

Circle each **f**.

d	f	p
f	g	g
f	c	f

Name:

Date:

Shadow Matching

Draw a line to the crown's matching shadow.

Name: ____________________ Date: ____________________

Count and Mark

Count the things in each box and mark the correct number.

7 1 6 2

2 4 5 8

2 3 5 9

8 4 9 3

Name: ______________________ Date: ______________________

Count and Mark

Count the things in each box and mark the correct number.

8 2 4 3

5 9 6 3

2 4 5 8

7 3 6 2

Name: ______________________ Date: ______________________

Trace and Write

Trace the lines to create the letter.

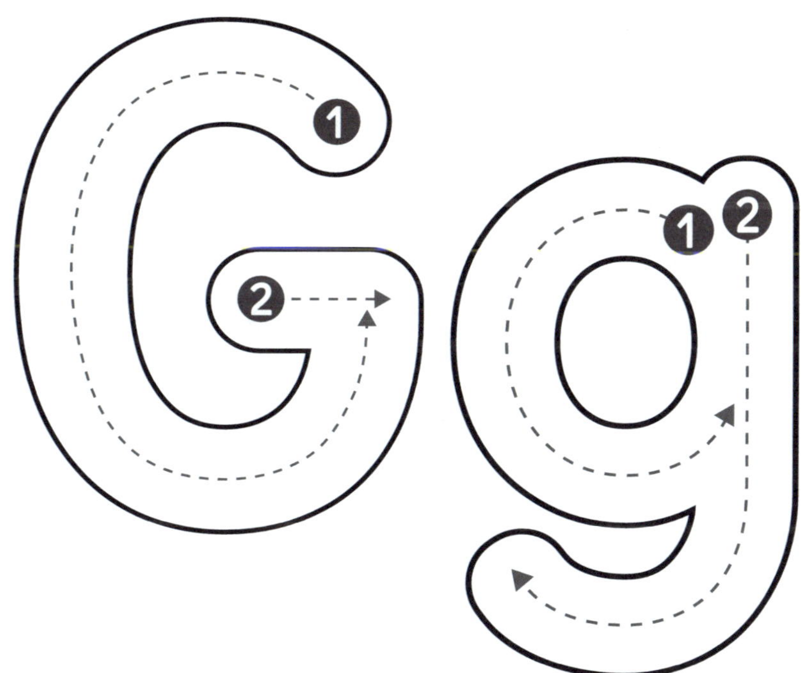

Circle each **G**.

P	J	G
G	G	P
G	C	D

Circle each **g**.

g	c	b
g	d	g
p	g	d

Name: ____________________ Date: ____________________

Where Is My Flower?

Trace the lines to help the butterflies get to their flower.

Name: ____________________ Date: ____________________

Tracing Letters

Practice writing the alphabet by tracing the letters below.

Name: ______________________ Date: ______________________

Tracing Circles

Trace the circles to help the mermaid blow all the bubbles!

Name:

Date:

Tracing ABC's

Trace the letters.

Name: ____________________ Date: ____________________

Trace and Write

Trace the lines to create the letter.

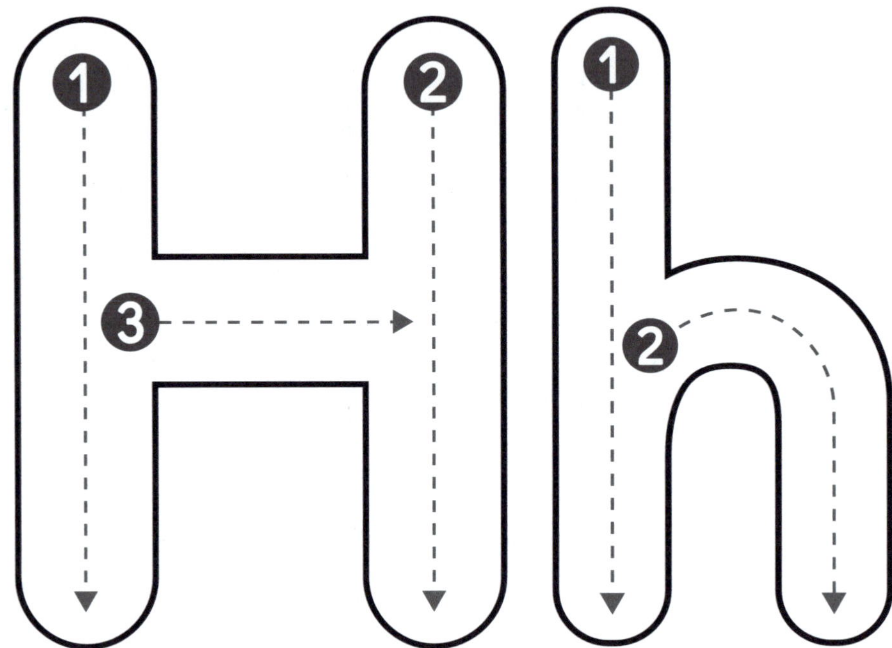

Circle each **H**.

G	C	H
D	H	P
H	D	H

Circle each **h**.

f	h	e
a	h	a
h	p	h

Name: ______________________ Date: ______________________

Tracing Triangles

Trace the triangles for the crown.

Name: ______________________ Date: ______________________

Circle The Color

Circle the friends that are blue.

Name: ______________________ Date: ______________________

Tracing ABC's

Trace the letters.

Name: _______________ Date: _______________

Read, Trace, Color

Trace the shapes then color them in.

Rectangle

Triangle

Square

Circle

Heart

Name:

Date:

Color Trace Draw

Name: ______________________ Date: ______________________

Trace and Write

Trace the lines to create the letter.

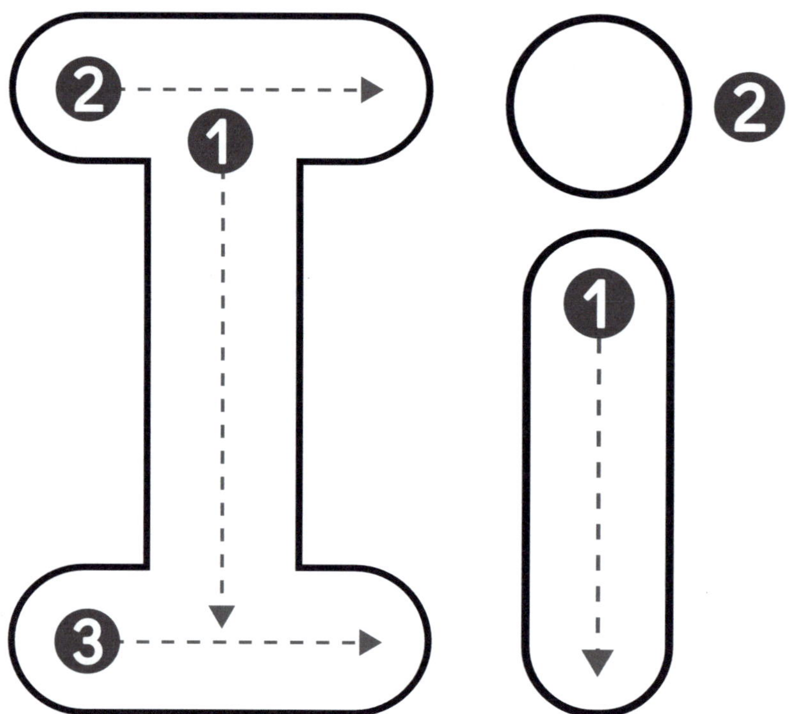

Circle each I.

I C P

I C P

L I O

Circle each i.

c i b

i g b

p c d

Name: ______________________ Date: ______________________

Tracing ABC's

Trace the letters.

Name: ____________________ Date: ____________________

Count and Mark

Count the things in each box
and mark the number.

4 3 7 5

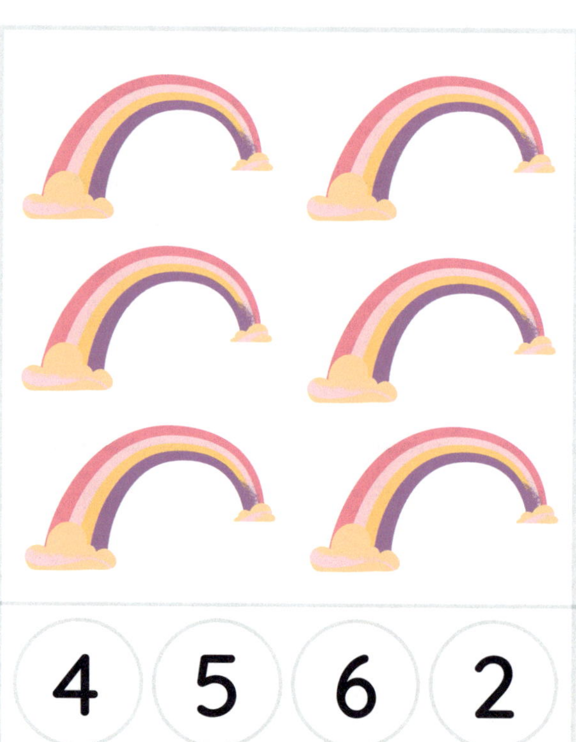

Name: ______________________ Date: ______________________

Color the Gg

Color the capital G's purple and lower case g's pink.

G	g	G	G	g	G	G
g	g	g	G	G	g	g
g	G	g	G	g	g	G
G	g	g	G	G	G	g
G	G	g	g	G	G	g
g	g	G	g	G	g	g
g	g	G	G	g	G	G
G	g	G	g	G	g	G
g	G	G	g	G	g	g

Name:

Date:

Trace and Write

Trace the lines to create the letter.

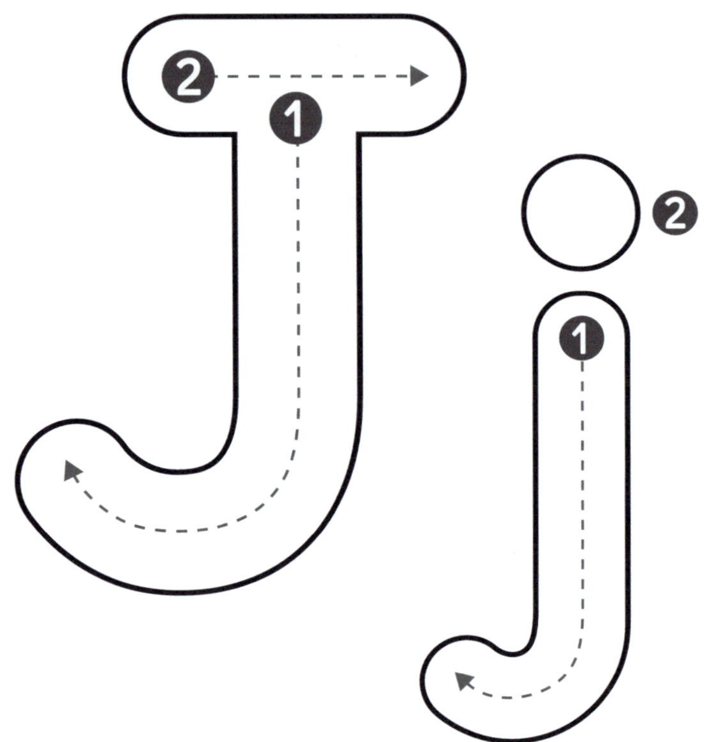

Circle each J.

H	J	M
J	J	D
P	C	J

Circle each j.

b	p	j
h	j	j
j	o	j

Name: ______________________ Date: ______________________

Tracing ABC's

Trace the letters.

Name:

Date:

Circle The Color

Circle the friends that are pink.

Name: ______________________ Date: ______________________

Trace and Write

Trace the lines to create the letter.

Circle each **K**.

B	K	K
P	H	K
K	K	G

Circle each **k**.

k	p	k
j	k	h
k	b	k

Name:

Date:

Tracing ABC's

Trace the letters.

Name: ______________________ Date: ______________________

Maze Fun!

Complete the maze to help the carriage get to the castle.

Name: ______________________ Date: ______________________

Trace and Write

Trace the lines to create the letter.

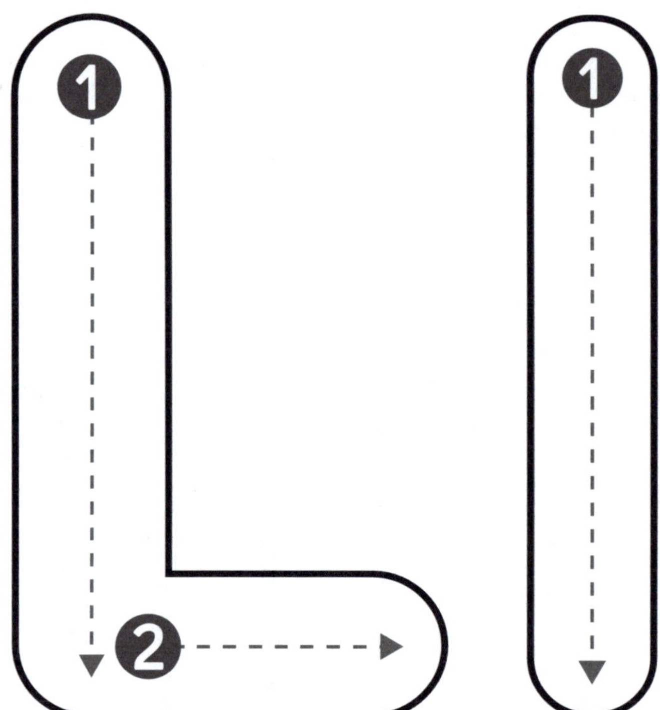

Circle each L.

L	J	L
P	L	S
J	L	G

Circle each l.

l	p	i
l	l	o
j	b	l

Name: ______________________________ Date: ______________________________

Color the Ll

Color the capital L's orange and lower case l's purple.

L L l L l l L

l l l L L L l

l L L l L l L

L l l L l L l

l L L l L l l

L l L l L l L

l l L L l L l

l L l l l L L

L L L l L L l

Name:

Date:

Tracing ABC's

Trace the letters.

U	U	U	U	U
V	V	V	V	V
W	W	W	W	W
X	X	X	X	X

Name:

Date:

Tracing Triangles

Trace the triangles to show the princess what triangles look like.

Name:

Date:

Trace and Write

Trace the lines to create the letter.

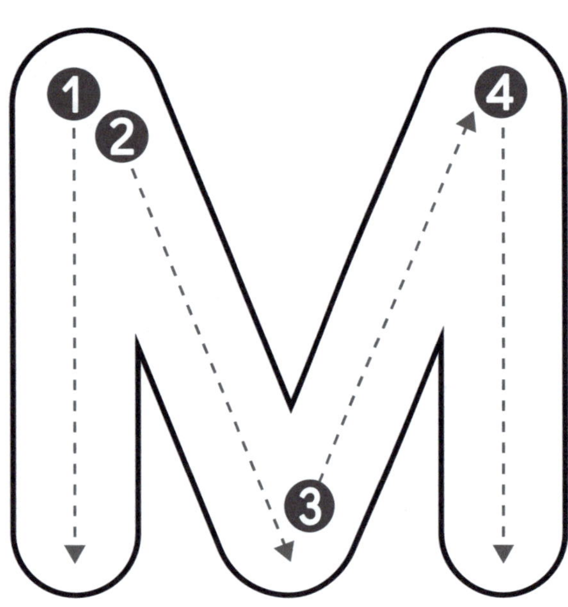

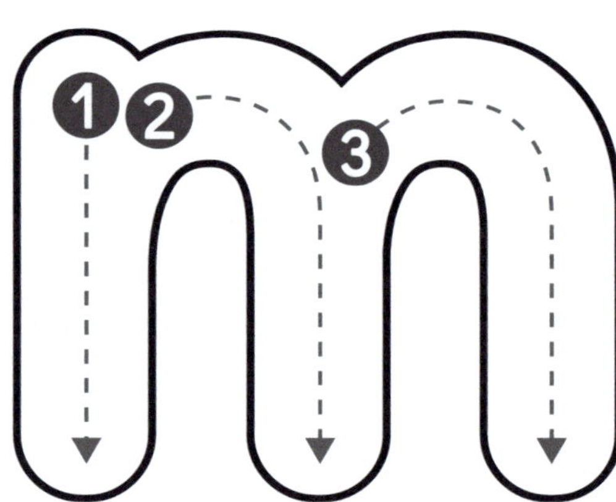

Circle each **M**.

T	M	B
M	K	M
J	H	M

Circle each **m**.

m	p	m
w	m	k
z	m	o

Name: ______________________ Date: ______________________

Maze Fun!

Complete the maze to help the unicorn get to the rainbow.

Name: ____________________ Date: ____________________

Color

Trace

Draw

Name: ______________________ Date: ______________________

Color the Mm

Color the capital M's green and lower case m's blue.

M	m	m	M	M	m	m
m	M	m	M	m	M	M
m	m	M	m	M	m	m
M	M	M	m	m	M	m
m	m	M	M	m	M	m
m	M	m	m	M	m	M
m	m	M	m	m	M	m
M	M	m	M	M	m	M
m	m	m	M	m	m	m

Name: ______________________ Date: ______________________

Trace and Write

Trace the lines to create the letter.

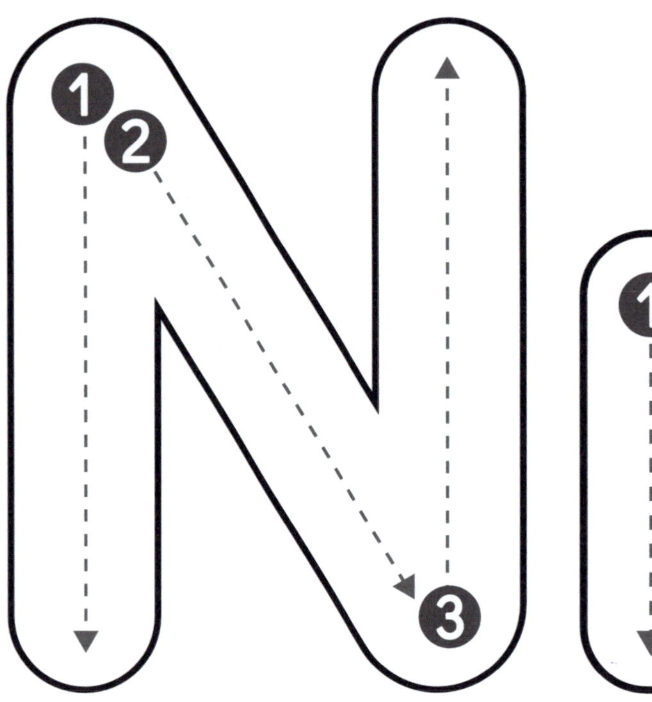

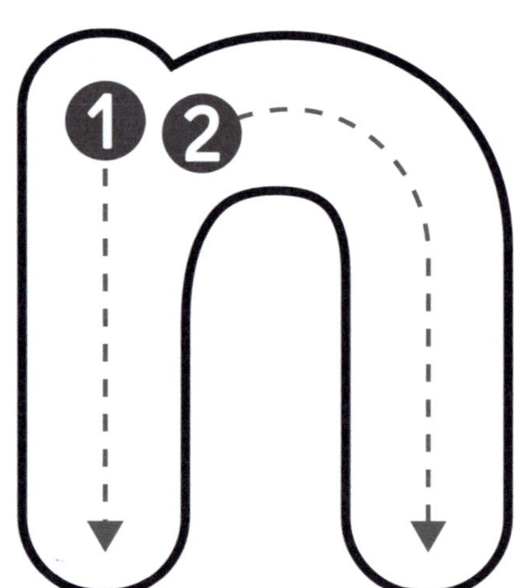

Circle each **N**.

N P U

J M N

N O N

Circle each **n**.

n w o

n c n

o o n

Name: ______________________ Date: ______________________

Maze Fun!

Complete the maze to help the princess find her crown.

Name: ______________________ Date: ______________________

Tracing Hearts

Trace the hearts to show how much the mermaids love their birthday party!

Name: ______________________ Date: ______________________

Trace and Write

Trace the lines to create the letter.

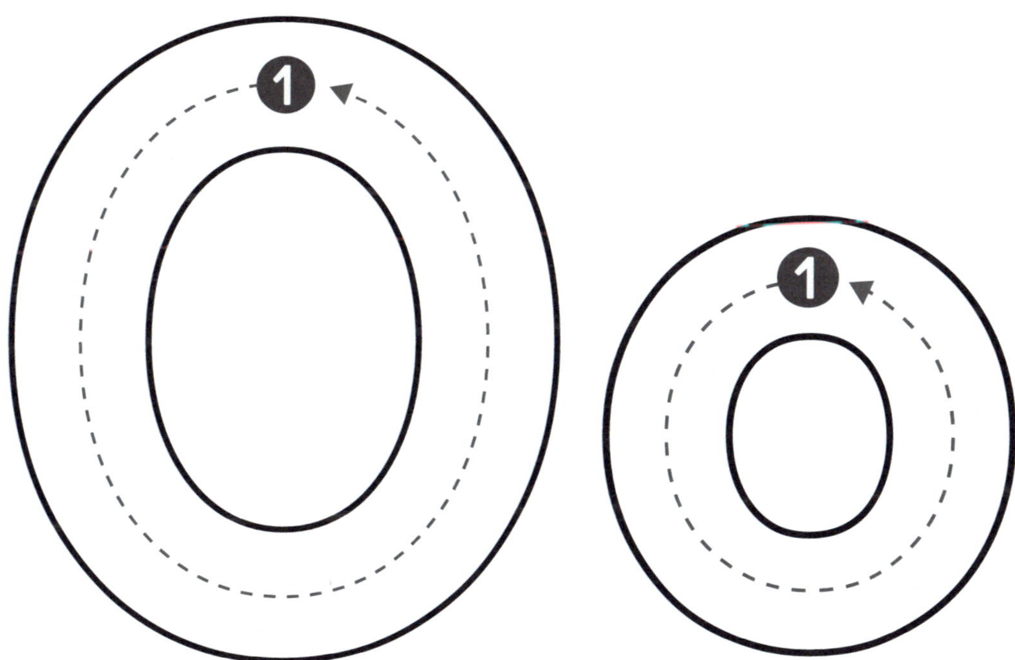

Circle each O.

O	P	U
J	M	O
N	O	N

Circle each o.

n	w	o
n	c	n
o	o	n

Name: ______________________ Date: ______________________

Maze Fun!

Complete the maze to help the fairy get to her house.

Name: ______________________ Date: ______________________

Circle The Color

Circle the friends that are yellow.

Name: ____________________ Date: ____________________

Trace and Write

Trace the lines to create the letter.

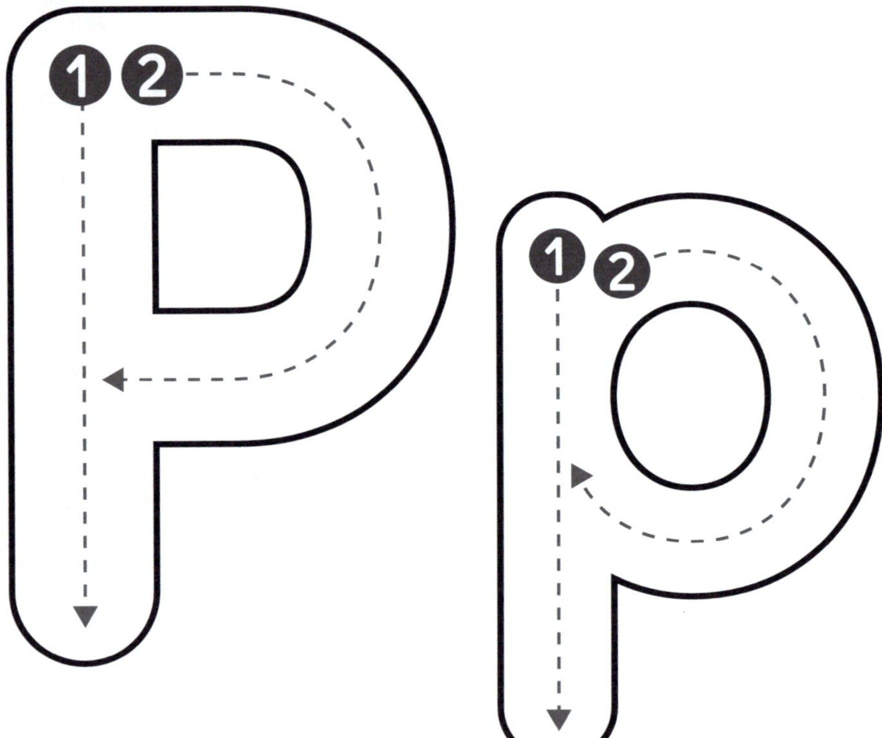

Circle each **P**.

M	U	P
P	O	D
P	P	U

Circle each **p**.

m	o	p
h	p	o
j	p	p

Name: ______________________ Date: ______________________

Tracing Shapes

Trace the shapes to help the fairies finish building their house.

Name: ______________________ Date: ______________________

Count and Circle

Circle the correct number of things.

4	
2	
5	
1	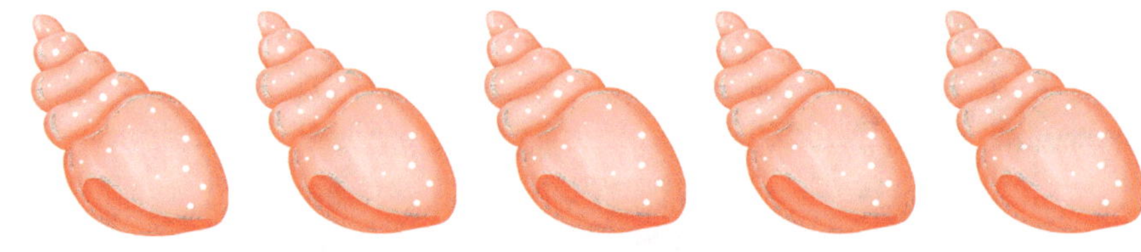
6	
3	

Name: ______________________ Date: ______________________

Trace and Write

Trace the lines to create the letter.

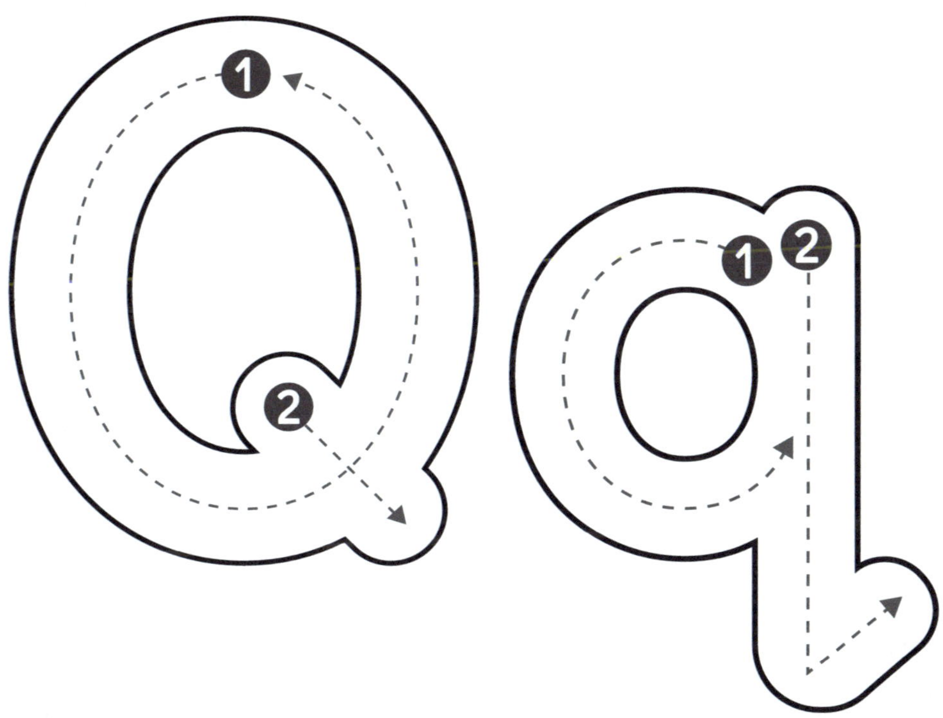

Circle each Q.

Q	P	U
J	M	Q
N	N	Q

Circle each q.

q	w	z
z	q	z
q	o	q

Name: ______________________ Date: ______________________

Shadow Matching

Draw a line to the house's matching shadow.

Name: ______________________ Date: ______________________

Circle The Color

Circle the friends that are green.

Name: ______________________ Date: ______________________

Spot the Qq

Color the capital Q's green and lower case q's blue.

Q q Q Q q q q
q q Q q Q q Q
Q Q q q q Q q
q q q Q q Q Q
q Q q Q q q Q
Q q Q Q q q q
q q Q q Q q Q
q Q Q Q q Q q
Q q Q Q Q q q

Name: ______________________ Date: ______________________

Trace and Write

Trace the lines to create the letter.

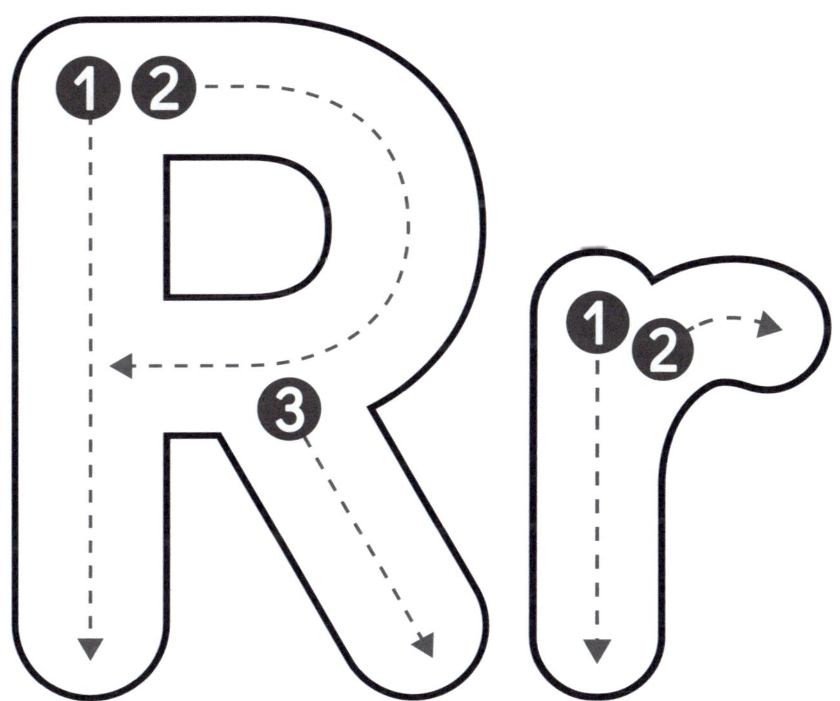

Circle each **R**.

Q	R	U
R	M	Q
N	R	Q

Circle each **r**.

r	w	r
z	r	r
q	o	r

Name: ______________________ Date: ______________________

Count and Mark

Count the things in each box and mark the correct number.

4 2 1 5

6 8 3 7

4 6 8 9

5 7 9 4

Name: ______________________ Date: ______________________

Circle The Color

Circle the friends that are red.

Name: ______________________ Date: ______________________

Color the Rr

Color the capital R's pink and lower case r's green.

r	R	r	r	R	r	r
R	R	R	r	R	R	R
r	r	R	R	r	R	r
r	R	r	R	r	r	R
R	r	r	R	r	R	r
r	R	r	r	R	r	R
r	r	R	R	r	R	r
r	R	r	r	R	R	R
R	R	r	r	R	r	r

Name: ______________________ Date: ______________________

Trace and Write

Trace the lines to create the letter.

Circle each S.

S	S	U
R	S	Q
S	R	Q

Circle each s.

r	s	r
s	s	u
q	s	r

Name:

Date:

Shape Matching

They are pretending to be yellow!
Draw a line to their match.

Name: ______________________ Date: ______________________

Maze Fun!

Complete the maze to help the mermaid find her seashell

Name: ______________________ Date: ______________________

Trace and Write

Trace the lines to create the letter.

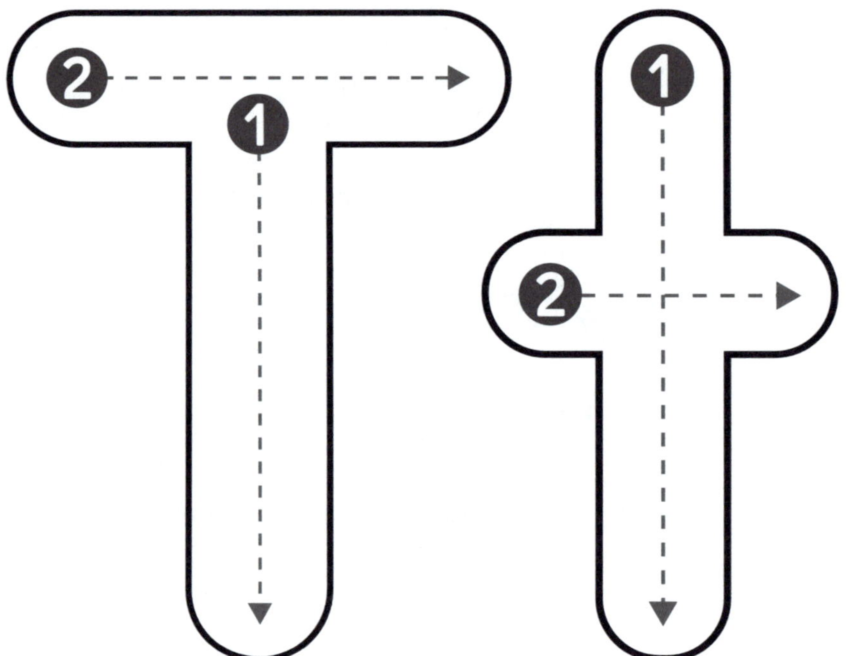

Circle each **T**.

S	T	T
R	S	T
T	R	Q

Circle each **t**.

r	b	t
t	s	u
t	t	r

Name: ____________________ Date: ____________________

Color the Tt

Color the capital T's yellow and lower case t's blue.

T t T t t T t

T T t t T t T

t t T t T t t

t t T T t T T

T T t T T t t

t t T t t t T

T T t t T t t

t T t t t T T

T t T T T t t

Name:

Date:

Count and Mark

Count the things in each box and mark the correct number.

5 8 3 9

1 2 5 4

3 4 6 8

3 4 2 5

Name: ____________________ Date: ____________________

Finish the Pattern

Draw the next shape on each line to finish the patterns.

Name: ______________________ Date: ______________________

Trace and Write

Trace the lines to create the letter.

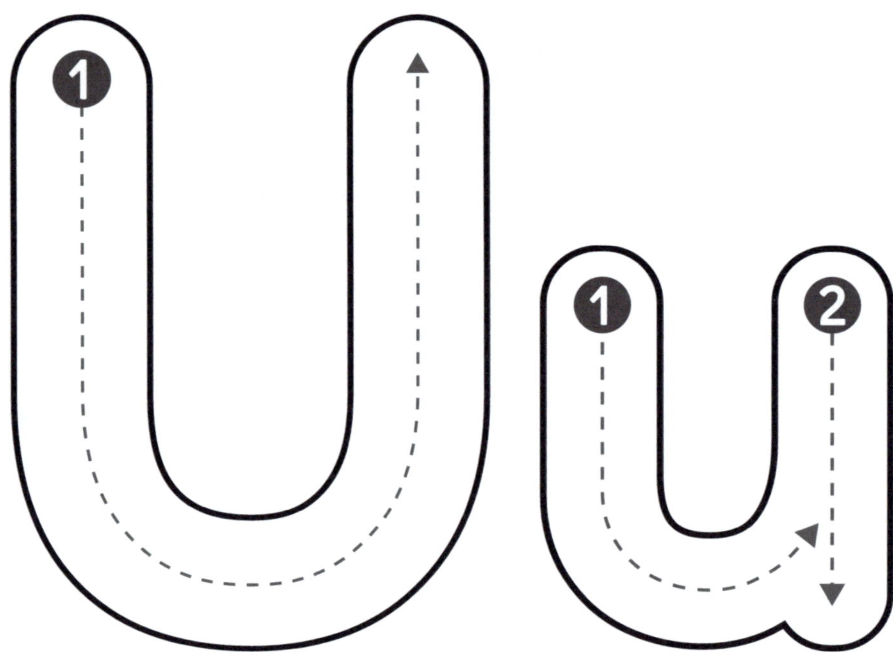

Circle each U.

U	U	T
B	S	T
T	U	Q

Circle each u.

r	u	t
u	s	u
t	u	u

Name: _______________ Date: _______________

Shadow Matching

Draw a line to the friends' matching shadows.

Name:

Date:

Maze Fun!

Complete the maze to help the unicorn get the princess to the party at the castle.

start →

end →

Name: ______________________ Date: ______________________

Tracing Rectangles

Trace the rectangles to teach the fairies what rectangles look like.

Name:

Date:

Trace and Write

Trace the lines to create the letter.

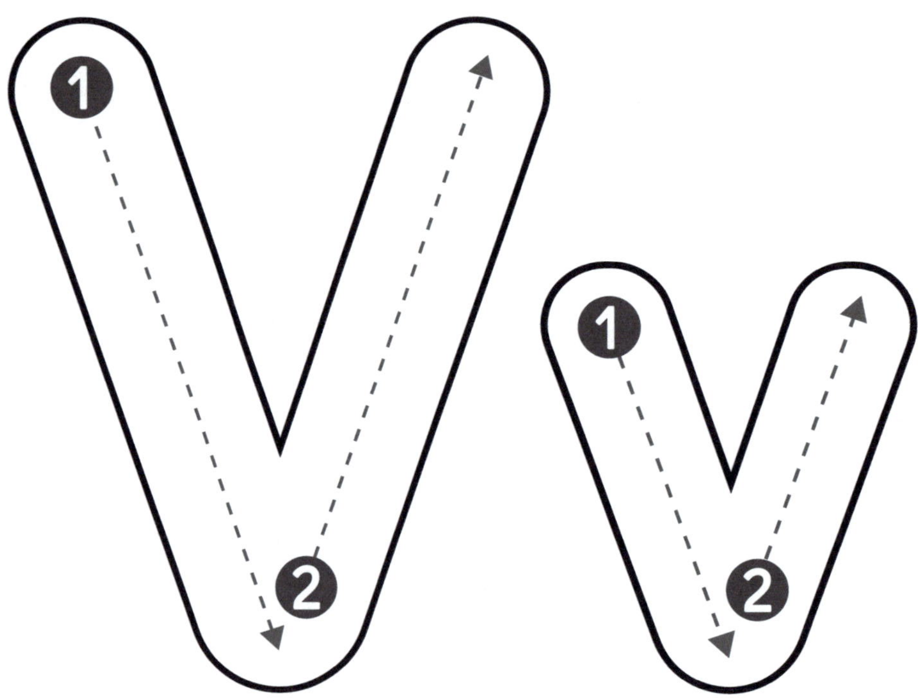

Circle each V.

V P U

J M V

N V N

Circle each v.

v w o

n v n

o v n

Name: ______________________ Date: ______________________

Tracing Lines

Trace the lines to help the mermaids to their seashell.

Name: ______________________ Date: ______________________

Circle The Color

Circle the vehicles that are purple.

Name: ______________________ Date: ______________________

Trace and Write

Trace the lines to create the letter.

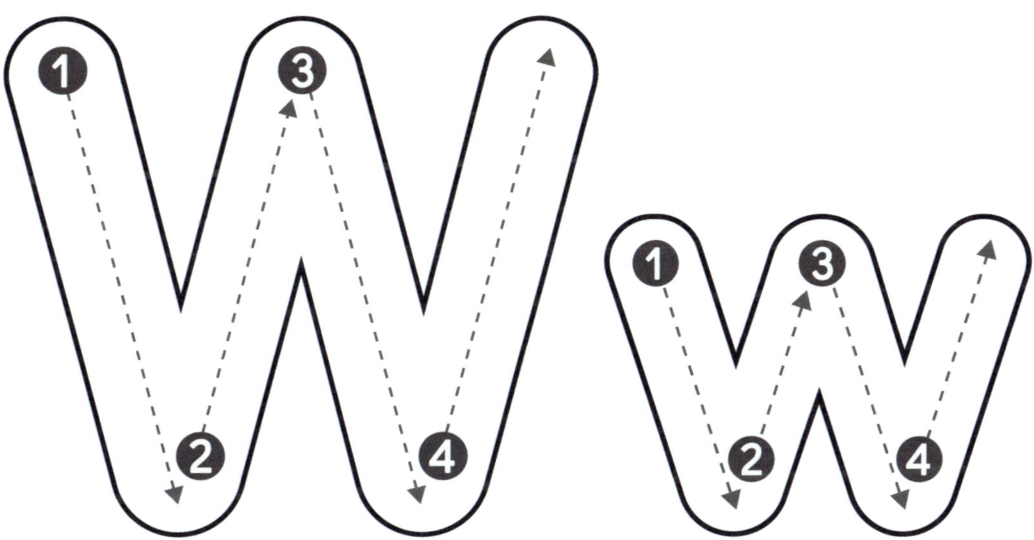

Circle each W.

W	U	T
B	W	T
T	W	Q

Circle each w.

w	w	t
u	w	o
t	u	w

Name:

Date:

Maze Fun!

Complete the maze to help the ballerina get to her new tutu.

Name: ______________________ Date: ______________________

Count and Circle

Circle the correct number of things.

1  

2 

3 

4 

5 

6 

Name:

Date:

Trace and Write

Trace the lines to create the letter.

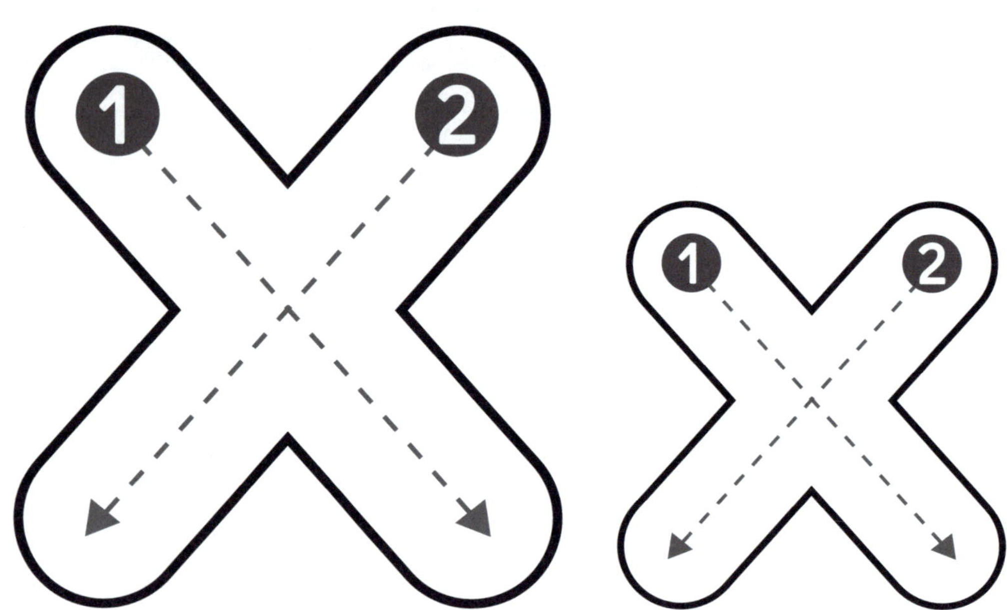

Circle each X.

W O X

X X T

F O X

Circle each x.

a x p

u x o

x b x

Name: ______________________ Date: ______________________

Tracing Numbers

Trace the numbers to complete the series.

1				
2				
3				
4		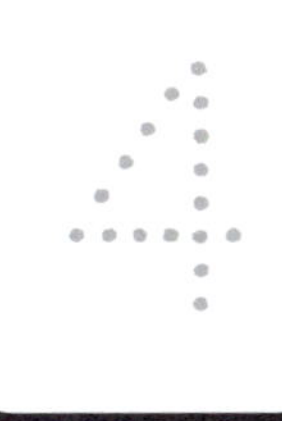		
5				

Name:

Date:

Tracing Numbers

Trace the numbers to complete the series.

Name: ______________________ Date: ______________________

Circle The Color

Circle the friends that are orange.

Name: ______________________ Date: ______________________

Star Numbers

Trace the numbers to count the stars.

Name: ______________________ Date: ______________________

Trace and Write

Trace the lines to create the letter.

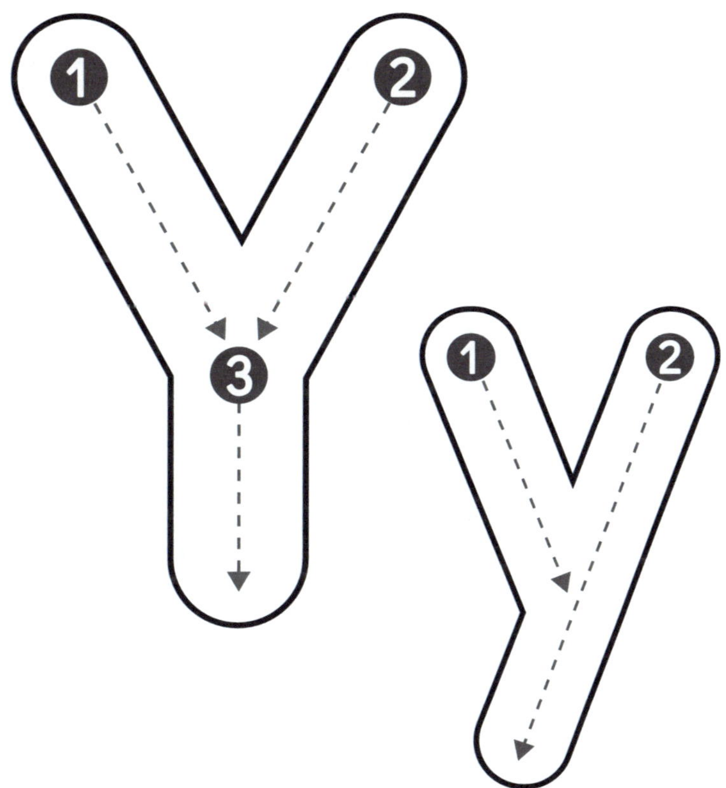

Circle each Y.

Y	A	Y
Y	T	T
F	A	Y

Circle each y.

a	y	p
u	y	y
o	b	y

Name: ____________________ Date: ____________________

Color the Yy

Color the capital Y's green and lower case y's purple.

y	Y	y	Y	y	Y	Y
y	y	Y	y	Y	Y	y
Y	Y	y	Y	Y	y	Y
Y	y	Y	y	y	y	y
y	Y	Y	Y	y	Y	Y
Y	Y	y	y	Y	Y	y
y	Y	y	Y	Y	y	y
Y	y	Y	y	Y	y	Y
y	Y	y	Y	y	Y	y

Name: ______________________ Date: ______________________

Tracing Numbers

Name:

Date:

Color Trace Draw

Name: ______________________ Date: ______________________

Trace and Write

Trace the lines to create the letter.

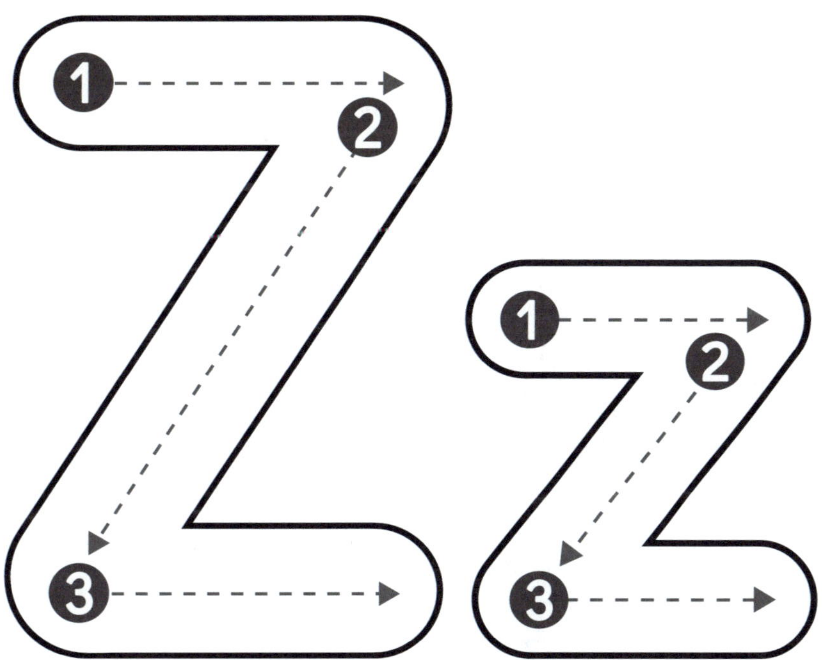

Circle each Z.

Z O X

X Z T

Z Z Z

Circle each z.

a z p

z x z

z b z

Name:

Date:

Finish the Pattern

Draw the next shape on each line to finish the pattern.

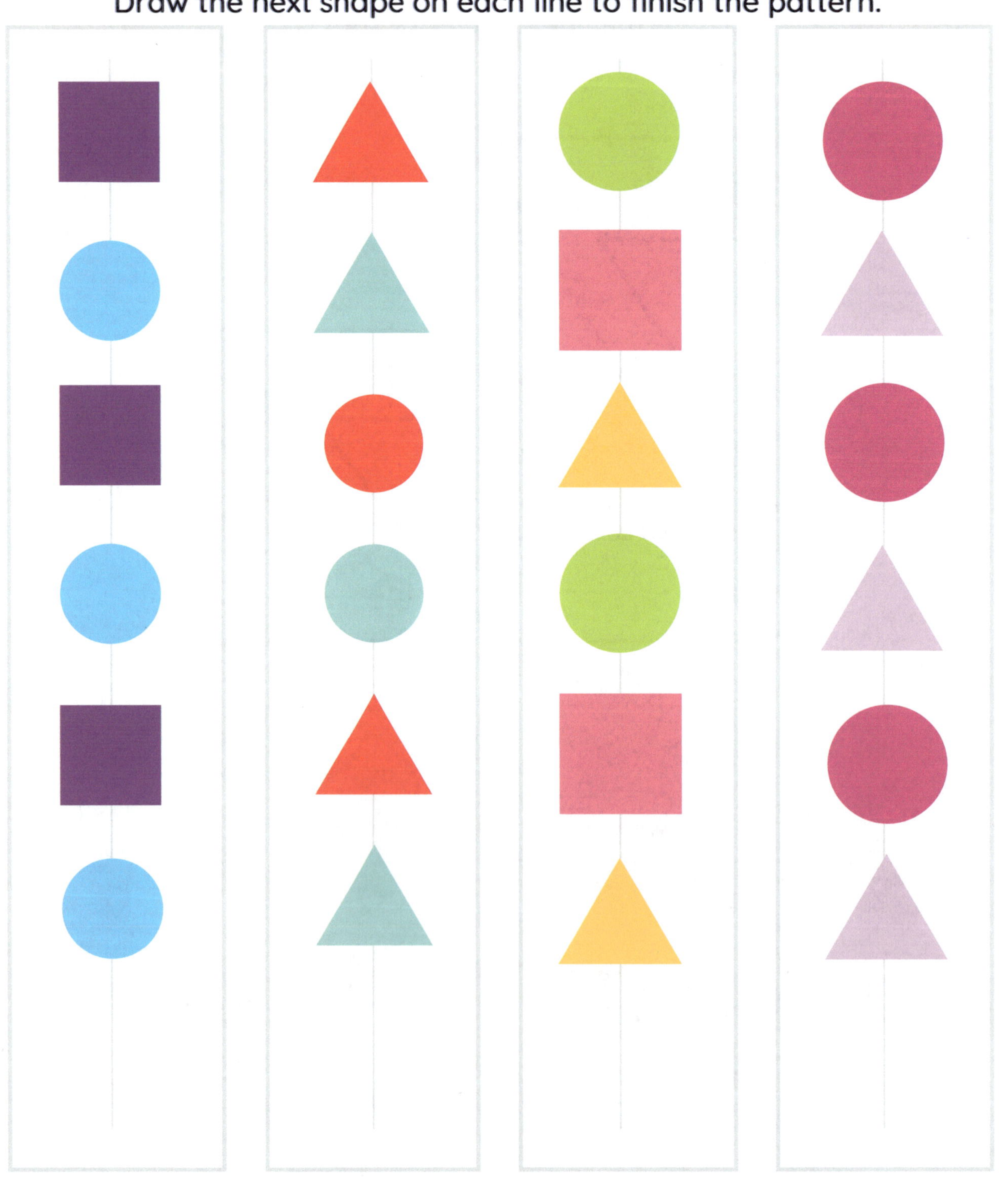

Name: ____________________ Date: ____________________

Star Numbers

Trace the numbers to count the stars.

Name: ______________________ Date: ______________________

Tracing ABC's

Trace the letters
to finish the ABC's.

Made in United States
Troutdale, OR
04/27/2024